T0326850

"As a pastor, I get asked lots of questions. I'm approached by unbelievers seeking to understand the gospel, new believers unsure about next steps, and maturing believers wanting help answering questions from their Christian family, friends, neighbors, or coworkers. It's in these moments that I wish I had a book to give them that was brief, answered their questions, and pointed them in the right direction for further study. Church Questions is a series that provides just that. Each booklet tackles one question in a biblical, brief, and practical manner. The series may be called Church Questions, but it could be called 'Church Answers.' I intend to pick these up by the dozens and give them away regularly. You should too."

Juan R. Sanchez, Senior Pastor, High Pointe Baptist Church, Austin, Texas

"Where can we Christians find reliable answers to our common questions about life together at church—without having to plow through long, expensive books? The Church Questions booklets meet our need with answers that are biblical, thoughtful, and practical. For pastors, this series will prove a trustworthy resource for guiding church members toward deeper wisdom and stronger unity."

Ray Ortlund, President, Renewal Ministries

Should I Be a Missionary?

Church Questions

Should
I Be a
Missionary?

Andy Johnson

:: CROSSWAY®

WHEATON, ILLINOIS

Should I Be a Missionary?

© 2024 by 9Marks

Published by Crossway
   1300 Crescent Street
   Wheaton, Illinois 60187

Cover image and design: Jordan Singer

First printing 2024

Printed in the United States of America

Trade paperback ISBN: 978-1-4335-9153-2
ePub ISBN: 978-1-4335-9155-6
PDF ISBN: 978-1-4335-9154-9

Library of Congress Cataloging-in-Publication Data

Names: Johnson, Andy, 1960- author.
Title: Should I be a missionary? / Andy Johnson.
Description: Wheaton, IL : Crossway, 2024. | Series: Church questions | Includes bibliographical references and index.
Identifiers: LCCN 2023052756 (print) | LCCN 2023052757 (ebook) | ISBN 9781433591532 (trade paperback) | ISBN 9781433591549 (pdf)
Subjects: LCSH: Missionaries—Vocational guidance.
Classification: LCC BV2061.3 .J63 2024 (print) | LCC BV2061.3 (ebook) | DDC 266.0023—dc23/eng/20240221
LC record available at https://lccn.loc.gov/2023052756
LC ebook record available at https://lccn.loc.gov/2023052757

Crossway is a publishing ministry of Good News Publishers.

BP			33	32	31	30	29	28	27	26	25	24
15	14	13	12	11	10	9	8	7	6	5	4	3	2	1

Go therefore and make disciples of all nations, baptizing them in the name of the Father and of the Son and of the Holy Spirit, teaching them to observe all that I have commanded you. And behold, I am with you always, to the end of the age.

Matthew 28:19–20

Ramona grew up in a town with a church building on every corner. Gospel-preaching churches seemed as easy to find as drive-thru restaurants. You might never pull in to order anything, but it was there if you wanted it. It had never occurred to her that the rest of the world might be different until she went on a church-sponsored mission trip to east Asia. During that trip, Ramona found herself surrounded by a level of spiritual poverty that she'd never seen before, and her perspective began to change.

One evening she looked down on a busy street from the balcony of her hotel. Contemplating the masses of people below, she found herself thinking, "There isn't a single gospel-preaching church in this city. Who is going to tell these people about Jesus? Maybe I should consider coming back to help establish a church. Maybe . . . I should be a missionary?"[1]

Do you have a similar story? Are you asking that same question? Or maybe someone who knows you gave you this booklet because they think you should be asking that question. Whatever the case, I hope to give you some Bible-based wisdom to help you along your way. And wherever you find yourself, I hope to help you get on with serving Jesus wherever you are and whatever your role in his church.

So let's get to it: Should you be a missionary?

Frankly, it depends.

It depends on your desires and giftings; it depends on the assessment of your church and church leaders; it depends on the opportunities presented to you; and it depends on a host of other factors as well that we'll explore in detail. Most importantly, it depends on whether you're genuinely a Christian.

I know that last comment might seem kind of obvious but it's the primary question you need to ask yourself: "Am I really a Christian?" If no, then your first concern should be your own alienation from God, not the alienation of the nations. You need to repent from your sin and trust in Christ's wrath-bearing death on the cross and resurrection from the dead for the forgiveness of sins. Making sure you're a Christian is far more important than asking whether you should be a missionary.

Now if you're confident that you are a Christian, you've still got a ways to go before deciding whether you should serve God overseas.

Should you be a missionary? Well, like I said, *it depends.*

1. It Depends on Whether You Understand What a Missionary Is and Does

Before you ask whether *you* should be a missionary, you need to be able to answer the question "What is a missionary?" It may surprise you, but in recent years Christians haven't always agreed on how to answer that question.

Some have suggested that since all Christians should obey Christ's command to make disciples, then it follows that all Christians are missionaries. I'll admit that's a tidy way to deal with the question. But that way of thinking essentially eliminates any unique meaning to the word "missionary." I once heard someone say, "If you underline every word in a book you're reading then you've underlined nothing." In the same way, if we think everyone is a missionary then the term becomes useless; it's just a slightly longer synonym for Christian.

Others think a missionary is any Christian living overseas or in another culture. But that way of thinking runs the risk of unwittingly ignoring the very real differences between Christians who have been commissioned and sent out for gospel work and Christians who just happen to be living internationally. The Bible clearly indicates that some Christians have been specially commissioned for missionary work.

For instance, the apostle John wrote about a special group of people whom he encouraged others to supply with resources because they had committed themselves to gospel work:

> You will do well to send them on their journey in a manner worthy of God. For they have gone out for the sake of the name, accepting nothing from the Gentiles. Therefore we ought to support people like these, that we may be fellow workers for the truth. (3 John 6–8)

John mentions people who were specially sent out for a gospel purpose and with a unique claim on the resources of the church. These were people whom Christians have traditionally called missionaries.

So let me be candid: No, not every Christian is a missionary. Also, simply being a Christian in a foreign context doesn't make you a missionary. A missionary has an identifiable commission, sent out from the church for a specific task.

But let's also consider what a missionary *does*.

Acts 13 contains one of the first and clearest examples of formally recognized, commissioned missionaries in Scripture. As some of the members and leaders of the Antioch church were worshiping the Lord, "The Holy Spirit said, 'Set apart for me Barnabas and Saul for the work to which I have called them.' Then after fasting and praying they laid hands on them and sent them off" (Acts 13:2–3).

Notice Barnabas and Paul were sent by the Holy Spirit *and by the local church* for a specific gospel work.

What did that work entail?

If you continue reading Acts you'll see that they were sent to do two primary things: (1) they were supposed to declare the good news of the gospel and make disciples, and (2) they were supposed to mark out true disciples by administering baptism and then incorporating those believers into biblically ordered local churches. Of course those things shouldn't surprise us. That's exactly what Jesus told the apostles to do in the Great Commission (Matt. 28:18–20).

You might be thinking: *That's interesting, those are the very things my church does in our community. We preach the gospel and baptize people into the church.* Exactly! A missionary is sent to do the work of the local church in a place where there is no church. The goal of the missionary then is to establish a local church so that the church can carry on that work for generations to come.

Interestingly, back in the 1600s a theologian named Gisbertus Voetius set out to define the work of a missionary according to Scripture. In the end he came up with a still famous "threefold" definition of the missionary task: The conversion of unbelievers; the planting of churches among the new believers; and, ultimately, the glorification and magnification of God's grace.[2]

Once that work has been accomplished, missionaries either continue serving those new local churches and supporting their ministries, or missionaries are sent to new places to plant new churches.

So should you be a missionary? It depends on whether you understand what a missionary is and the work that missionaries do.

But that's not it. You still have more to consider.

2. It Depends on Whether You Meet the Qualifications for a Lead Missionary

Robert is passionate about evangelism, and he can't escape the idea that maybe he should be a missionary. True, he doesn't know his Bible very well, and he's not exactly the kind of guy that other Christians go to for mature counsel. But he loves people deeply, he's personable, outgoing, and willing to go overseas. He also loves international food and other cultures. Plus, people like him—oh, and did I mention he's willing to go overseas?

Should Robert be a missionary? To answer that question we again need to look to the Bible.

The Bible describes *two types* of missionaries: (1) highly-qualified church planters, and (2) the men and women who help them. Take for example Barnabas in the New Testament. He wasn't an apostle like Paul, but he seems to have been a "lead" missionary sent out by the church in Antioch.

One particular account in Acts makes that point clearly. Paul and Barnabas were ministry partners, but they eventually parted ways over a disagreement about whether John Mark should be allowed to join their team. Barnabas went to plant a church in Cyprus, while Paul ministered to already existing churches in Syria (Acts 15:36–41).

Scripture doesn't tell us who was right and who was wrong. But perhaps one of the reasons the Holy Spirit included this story in Scripture was to make clear that the work of planting churches wasn't just for apostles like Paul. That work could be carried out even by ordinary, mature, qualified guys like Barnabas (and maybe like you too!)

Stories like this one show that missionary teams in the New Testament were led by at least one mature, godly man who knew the Bible well and was able to teach others. One might refer to these leading missionaries as "elder-qualified" men. These are men who could plant a church *and* pastor it.

The qualifications for elders in 1 Timothy 3 and Titus 1 are particularly important here. If you've not read those passages recently let me encourage you to stop right now and read them. According to Scripture, pastors (also called elders) must be two things: (1) faithful men of godly character who can model obedience to God for their fellow Christians (1 Pet. 5:3), and (2) men able to teach God's word so that Christians can learn to obey everything that Jesus commanded (1 Tim. 3:2; Titus 1:9).

Paul says as much to his protégé Timothy. Timothy was Paul's church-planting assistant. But Paul left him in Ephesus to be the lead missionary and continue pastoring the church that they planted (1 Tim. 1:3). In 2 Timothy 2:1–2, Paul instructed Timothy about the importance of raising up more men like himself:

> You then, my child, be strengthened by
> the grace that is in Christ Jesus, and what

you have heard from me in the presence
of many witnesses entrust to *faithful* men,
who will be able to *teach* others also.

What two priorities does Paul set out for fu-
ture missionaries and pastors? Faithfulness and
the ability to teach others—the two dominant
characteristics of an elder-qualified man.

Consider each of those two elements.

What does *faithfulness* look like in a missionary context? It looks like holding on to the truth,
come what may. A faithful witness is one who
keeps telling the message of the gospel without
wavering. If people ignore the message, a faithful
witness won't try to change the message to make
it more interesting, transferable, or palatable.
Knowing what you have been told to do and to
say, and having the patience to keep on doing
and saying only what you have been told, is the
mark of faithfulness.

What about the *ability to teach*? A faithful
lead missionary is someone who knows what
the Bible says about the gospel, the church, and
the Christian life and who can communicate

those truths to others. They understand what God achieved in the person and work of Christ for the salvation of sinners. They have a clear understanding of how the gospel spreads through faithful gospel proclamation and discipling in the context of local churches. They understand that every human idea, scheme, and method is not necessarily consistent with Scripture's ministry methodology. In short, they know what the Bible says, and they stick with it.

How do we identify lead missionaries? A good place to look would be within the elders of your local church. The kind of men that a wise church would choose to be its own elders are probably the kind of men they should be sending out as lead missionaries. Does this mean that every lead missionary must be, or have been, a local church elder? No, I wouldn't go that far. But I think the men we send to *lead* missionary efforts should be similarly qualified. Given what faithful missions work looks like, why wouldn't this be the case?

3. It Depends on Your Ability to Help a Lead Missionary

Of course, lead missionaries aren't the only people local churches send out. Along with those men, the biblical authors speak about co-workers or "helpers" (Acts 19:22) who provide invaluable assistance to the lead missionary or missionaries.

For instance, in Acts 18 we read of a couple, Priscilla and Aquila, who became some of Paul's most trusted associates. Paul valued their help on his "team" so much that when he left Corinth he took them with him to help his missionary work elsewhere: "After this, Paul stayed many days longer and then took leave of the brothers and set sail for Syria, and with him Priscilla and Aquila" (Act 18:18).

As we saw earlier, Paul and Barnabas took helpers with them to be on their teams after they parted from each other:

> Barnabas took Mark with him and sailed away to Cyprus, but Paul chose Silas and departed, having been commended by the

brothers to the grace of the Lord. (Acts 15:39–40)

Alongside a lead missionary, these helpers play a vital role. Some eventually become elder-qualified themselves and are able to lead their own church planting efforts. Barnabas, Timothy, and Titus are examples of such men. Others continue to assist lead missionaries as coworkers or helpers for their entire lives—saints like Silas, Priscilla, and John Mark.

So if church planting efforts should be led by at least one elder-qualified man, does Scripture give any qualifications for these "helper" missionaries? Not quite. The Bible doesn't provide a specific list of qualifications for missionary helpers in the same way it does for elders. Nevertheless, we can arrive at a few guiding principles from Scripture and apply a bit of sanctified common sense.

Since these helpers will be on the front lines of ministry, these men and women should have at least an above average maturity in most areas of the Christian life. They should also have at least an above average knowledge of the Bible and the ability to apply it to their lives and the lives of others. As evidenced by Paul's concern with John Mark, they should be people who demonstrate consistent faithfulness.

They should also be men and women who understand the importance of the local church—after all, the whole point of missions is establishing healthy local churches. Most significantly, they should be the type of people that an elder-qualified missionary would want as helpers. If an elder-qualified man thinks a sister or brother in Christ would be an aid to their work, that speaks volumes about whether they're ready for the task.

One practical tool you could use to evaluate men and women for this role would be the qualifications for deacons listed in 1 Timothy 3:8–13. While these helpers may or may not have been formally affirmed as deacons, they should be deacon-like. It's hard to imagine asking a church to support someone who does not fulfill every quality mentioned in Paul's list.

What about you? Could you help or support a lead missionary? Would others in your church agree? Supporting roles are critical for the missionary enterprise. Maybe that could be a role for you.

4. It Depends on Your Willingness to Be Patient and Stick to God's Plan

Ministry is challenging. It requires slow, patient work as we trust God to produce fruit to the degree he chooses in the timing he chooses. Sadly, the history of Christian missions is littered with examples of impatient missionaries who gave up on biblical principles to embrace "better" ways of doing ministry—methods that promised fast, visible results. You may not know any of their names because in most cases their work fizzled out.

At the same time, you might recognize the names of men like William Carey and Adoniram Judson whose missionary work was marked by faithfulness and patience. Judson labored at translating and teaching the Bible for seven years before he saw his first convert. Some estimate that he only saw about eighteen converts during his entire life's ministry in Burma. But the church remembers Judson not for his flashy results, but because he patiently stuck to the hard, simple work of preaching the gospel and teaching people to obey everything that Jesus commanded. Two centuries later the echo of his faithful labor is heard in the songs of tens of thousands of Christians in hundreds of local churches throughout Southeast Asia.

So what ministry plan should missionaries patiently pursue?

In sum, they need to preach a biblical gospel teaching disciples to obey everything that Jesus commanded in the context of a local church that's ordered by God's commands in Scripture.

Is that a plan you can stick with for years even if you don't see any visible fruit? If so, then God might be fitting you to be a missionary.

Missionaries must love others enough to pour out their lives for others. They don't merely see others as potential workers for more missions efforts (1 Thess. 2:8); they must teach everything that Jesus commanded, not just the inoffensive bits (Matt. 28:20); they must declare the gospel, not a modified, culturally appealing version of it (2 Cor. 4:2); they must pray and rely on God's power to save, not on manmade schemes, methods, or programs (1 Cor. 2:1–5); they must gather believers into biblically ordered churches, not just quickly assembled Bible study groups (Titus 1:5); they must train up leaders in sound doctrine, not just have them memorize a few Bible stories (2 Tim. 2:2); and they must do these things for as long as God allows or decrees, trusting that their labor is never in vain (1 Cor. 15:58).

Again I want to be candid: if you're not willing to work hard, stick to that plan, and patiently wait for God to bring the harvest in his own good time (1 Cor. 3:5–6) then *please, please, please do not become a missionary!* Missionaries who turn to theologically careless models of ministry that promise quick results and rapid multiplication often do more harm than good on the mission field. They confuse lots of lost people about what it really means to be a Christian. They often leave in their wake hundreds, if not thousands, of people who have been assured that they're going to heaven without any evidence of genuine faith.

These rapid-multiplication missions methods have constantly changing names—"Church Planting Movements," "Rapidly Advancing Discipleship," and "Disciple-Making Movements" are some recent iterations. Frankly, the names seem to change each time the previous "golden method" loses momentum. But the basic ideas sadly stay the same. Instead of advocating that missionaries patiently teach God's word and carefully order local churches, these methods employ techniques that promise bigger, faster, easier results. They often ignore the centrality of the local church altogether; after all, healthy local churches take far too long to establish. They diminish the importance of sound doctrine (again, it takes too long to teach). They ignore the biblical warnings against appointing unqualified leaders because training qualified leaders wouldn't be rapid. It shouldn't surprise us that Westerners who gave the world fast-food restaurants and network marketing would apply those values and principles to the work of missions—to disastrous results.

Instead, missionaries need to follow Bible-saturated wisdom of pastors like Charles Bridges. A century before the advent of "movement" methodologies and ministry fads promising "rapid" results, Pastor Bridges recognized that impatience might lead good men into unwitting unfaithfulness. He wrote:

> Our plain and cheering duty is therefore to go forward—to scatter the seed, to believe and to wait. Yet must there be expectancy as well as patience. . . . Faith and patience will be exercised—sometimes severely so. But after a painstaking, weeping seed-time, we shall bring our sheaves with rejoicing, and lay them upon the altar of God. . . . Meanwhile we must beware of saying— "Let him make speed, and hasten his work that we may see it." The measure and the time are with the Lord. We must let Him alone with His own work. Ours is the care of service—His is the care of success. The

Lord of the harvest must determine when, and what, and where the harvest shall be.[3]

Again, if you're tempted to be impatient in ministry, if you're tempted to look for shortcuts and engineer results, if you have a hard time not despising the day of small beginnings, then please, for the sake of the nations, stay where you are, keep maturing in your local church, and help your church support missionaries ready for the trials of slow, patient ministry. Real faithfulness is hard. Like Judson, we may see little fruit in our lifetimes, but that doesn't mean God doesn't have a plan for the years to come.

If you begrudge trusting God to grant fruit in his own time you're not ready to be a missionary. But if that truth delights you and thrills your soul, then you might be a missionary-in-the-making. After all, the fact that God sovereignly works as we patiently follow his ways should be profoundly encouraging and liberating. One of the reasons I'm currently laboring in the place where I now serve is because I know that my ministry doesn't all rely on me—on my methods, my creativity, and my strategies. I'm exhilarated by the knowledge that even a messed-up guy like me can bear fruit if I just stick to the simple pattern of ministry laid out in Scripture. By persevering, working hard, loving my church, and letting the life of the church community commend the gospel, I have great hope for what God might do through me and through our church—even if I don't live to see the fruit he brings.

How about you? If the thought of faithfully persevering and relying on God encourages you, missions might be for you too. Hope in God is the soil in which the seed of patience grows best. We know that for those who remain faithful, God will show himself gracious, faithful, and sufficient. Test him, obey his word, and persevere. He alone knows what fruit we may reap in years to come if we remain faithful and don't give up (Gal. 6:9).

5. It Depends on Your Desire to Be Sent

All Christians want to see the gospel reach the lost and Christ's glory exalted among the nations. But simply desiring to see Christ exalted among the nations is just a sign that you're a healthy Christian who loves Jesus; it's not a sign that you should be a missionary.

Let me be even more specific: if you don't have a personal desire to be sent to a different culture to do gospel-focused work, then you absolutely should not be a missionary—at least not yet. Churches shouldn't ever send *unwilling* missionaries.

At the same time, the desire to serve as a missionary can look different for different kinds of people. I have known some folks for whom the desire to be sent out was an almost overpowering, consuming passion. I've known others, more like myself, for whom becoming a missionary simply involved learning about particular needs, having a willingness to fill them, and a providential opportunity to meet those needs. I certainly didn't experience any blinding lights on a Damascus road like Paul.

Desire alone isn't sufficient, but it is important.

For this reason, I worry that some of the ways that Christian leaders have encouraged missionary service are actually unhelpful and misleading.

For instance, I've heard well-meaning preachers tell scores of young people things like: "You don't need a reason to go, you need a reason to stay." That makes for a catchy sound bite, but it's poor advice for young Christians. For one thing it doesn't properly respect the doctrine of Christian liberty; you don't have to be a missionary to honor Jesus. It also doesn't give proper respect to the importance and difficulty of missionary work. We don't just need more warm bodies called missionaries; we need qualified people sent by healthy churches who are equipped to do missions well.

So as you think about your own desires, let me offer two wrong motivations for desiring to be a missionary and one right motivation for missionary work.

Wrong Motivation 1: Uninformed Enthusiasm

Sometimes enthusiasm for missions can just be misguided idealism or a longing for adventure.

I've even seen folks desire missionary work so they could "reinvent" themselves in a new place, especially if their season of life seemed dull or if bad decisions had made life unpleasant. Obviously these are bad reasons to pursue missionary work.

More positively sometimes Christians desire to do missions because they genuinely love Jesus and want to see him exalted in the nations, but they don't yet have a clear grasp on the teachings of Scripture or on the missionary task itself. If that's you, realize your desires are not bad. They're wonderful! But you need to spend time learning more about the character needed to serve as a missionary and the work that missionaries do on the field. As you pursue that knowledge, see if your desire wanes or if it persists and grows. Talking to a mature Christian in your church who has experience with overseas missionary work would be a great place to start. Don't just assume that a sudden desire is God's leading. It could be the start of something, but you need to test that desire with knowledge.

Wrong Motivation 2: Guilt-Motivated Obligation

You should also be careful if your desire to be a missionary is fueled by a sense of guilt or obligation. I've known a few Christians who didn't really want to be missionaries but because they had grown up overseas and spoke a strategic language fluently, they reasoned that they *ought* to be missionaries—even though the idea made them mildly nauseous.

If you're considering missions out of guilt or obligation you should seek out an elder or another mature Christian in your church and talk to them about it. A wise friend can help you sort through your emotions. You might need to be challenged to continue on the path; maybe you're hesitating out of fear. On the other hand, you might need just to be told to chill-out and embrace the freedom you have in Christ. You don't *have* to be a missionary, no matter what background God has given you.

Right Motivation: Gospel-Inspired Willingness

Some of you reading this book might not resonate with either of those wrong motivations.

Instead, your desires grow as you learn more about the missionary task and as you become more aware of gospel needs around the world. You realize that you are free in Christ to choose any number of faithful paths; but this path—the path of missions—just persists in your thoughts and affections.

Or it could be that you simply recognize that you might be particularly suited to the work of missions, the need is great, you'd enjoy the work, so why not go? Whether your desire is white-hot and wise or cool and sober, if your love for the gospel is driving you toward the nations, then you need to seriously consider taking steps in that direction. Again, you should seek out a pastor or elder in your church and talk to them about your desires soon.

Before moving on, let me give a few quick caveats if you're thinking about this question and you're already married. If you're a married man, have you spoken to your wife about your desires? Is she willing to happily follow you in this path? Have you asked her directly . . . several times? Conversely, if you're a married woman and your husband is leading in this direction, do you also have a personal desire for this life? Can you happily follow your husband into missionary life? If not, it's much better to be honest about that now rather than later.

If you're a married woman desiring missions, does your husband have a leading desire for missions as well? Or are you pushing him in a direction beyond his desire to lead? If you need help working through some of these questions, meet with a pastor in your church to discuss them.

In sum, you need to desire to be a missionary but you also need to carefully test your desires. Consider not only *if* you want to be a missionary but why. Finally, recognize that mature desire often focuses more on the outcome, not on the thing itself. I may genuinely desire to exercise, not because I love exercise itself, but because I want what it will produce—greater health and the ability to button my jeans again. Similarly Christians don't ultimately desire the missionary life (the Bible paints it as a pretty tough road; check out 2 Corinthians 11:25–26) but they desire what it will produce—the potential for redeemed souls and new churches glorifying God among the nations. If you desire to be a part of that work on the front lines, talk to your church's leaders about being a missionary.

6. It Depends on Your Church's Desire to Send You

You might have a desire to be sent, but does your church desire to send you?

Before we continue I should warn you that some churches can be pretty careless when it comes to appointing folks to missionary work. Frankly if you're in a church that would send anyone who is willing to go, then you may need to work harder to get an honest assessment of your fitness for missions work. Talk to your church leaders and try to get them to engage your desires with seriousness and sobriety. Ask them to test you and give you honest feedback. If you don't think they will do this seriously, thoughtfully, and courageously (being willing to tell you "no" or "not yet"), then you should probably seek out a more faithful church.

Ultimately, you shouldn't be a self-sent missionary. You want a faithful local church to know you deeply, test your gifts, and affirm you either as a lead missionary or as a qualified helper. Sadly, many prospective missionaries today resist this kind of intentional assessment. Those who do almost always follow a disastrous path of being self-sent missionaries, even if ostensibly commissioned by some detached church or organization.

Interestingly, the best example of the danger of "self-sent" missionaries doesn't come from the modern missions movement but from the pages of Scripture. Acts 15 tells us the story:

> But some men came down from Judea and were teaching the brothers, "Unless you are circumcised according to the custom of Moses, you cannot be saved." And after Paul and Barnabas had no small dissension and debate with them, Paul and Barnabas and some of the others were appointed to go up to Jerusalem to the apostles and the elders about this question. (Acts 15:1–2)

Paul and Barnabas eventually made it to Jerusalem and went straight to the church leaders and reported these unauthorized missionaries. The elders of the Jerusalem church sent the following letter back to the believers at Antioch.

> The brothers, both the apostles and the elders, to the brothers who are of the Gentiles in Antioch and Syria and Cilicia, greetings. Since we have heard that some persons have gone out from us and troubled you with words, unsettling your minds, although we gave them no instructions, it has seemed good to us, having come to one accord, to choose men and send them to you with our beloved Barnabas and Paul, men who have risked their lives for the name of our Lord Jesus Christ. (Acts 15:23–26)

These troublesome, unauthorized "missionaries" went out on their own. Because of the mess they made, the elders in Jerusalem "sent" Paul and Barnabas, along with Judas and Silas (Acts 15:27), to clean up the mess.

In short, don't do what the self-sent guys from Jerusalem did. Don't be an unauthorized, mess-making missionary.

Once again, make yourself known to your church leaders. Make them aware that you are considering the question, "Should I be a missionary?" Ask them for help. Look for opportunities to let them equip, train, and test you. Be willing to listen to them and patiently wait for them to affirm whether you're ready for missionary work or not. The good of your soul and of countless others may be deeply impacted by your humility or arrogance in this regard.

7. It Depends on Your Love for What Jesus Loves

Tom is an enthusiastic and sincere Christian. He's passionate about sharing the gospel with others and quick to get involved in gospel work in the community. He isn't particularly faithful to his local church—in fact, he's never even joined the church he attends. He says he's simply too busy; joining with a local church doesn't contribute to his ministry. Most of the people there aren't as mature and serious as he is (or so he thinks), and he's convinced the church would limit labors for the gospel. Now Tom is thinking about becoming a missionary.

What do you think? Should Tom be a missionary?

If the work of the missionary is primarily to preach the gospel and to gather believers into local churches, then sending out workers who lack a demonstrated love for Christ's church makes little, if any, sense. It's like letting someone adopt children who only cares about getting parental rights, but doesn't care about nurturing the children afterward. Christians who don't love Jesus's church *might* love Jesus (though the Bible casts doubt on that—1 John 4:20–21) but they certainly don't love what Jesus loves.

Jesus loves his church. He desires to build his church. As Paul says in Ephesians 5:

> Christ loved the church and gave himself up for her, that he might sanctify her, having cleansed her by the washing of water

with the word, so that he might present
the church to himself in splendor, without
spot or wrinkle or any such thing, that she
might be holy and without blemish. (Eph.
5:25–27)

The work of Jesus was all about winning and
blessing his church. People who don't love what
Jesus loves shouldn't become missionaries.

This point may sound obvious, but sadly it's
not. Many of the "missionaries" in the central
Asian city where I pastor show little love for
the local church. Even though missionaries
here are free to gather with churches and even
though there are gospel-preaching churches
that speak the native language of these missionaries, many still don't bother to join a
church. They're far more committed to their
missionary team than to a local congregation.
The irony of course is that many of these missionaries claim that they are in our area to plant
a church! Why they'd be so interested in planting churches and so disinterested in joining
one is troubling.

One way to assess if you should be a missionary is to look at your life right now and ask "Do I love what Jesus loves? Do I love the local church?"

Are you committed to a local church and have you built your life around it? Do you understand the importance of church membership and discipline? Does your desire for missions include a desire to lock arms with expat and local Christians in the place you'll be serving? If the answer to those questions is yes, then you might be someone who should be thinking about doing missions.

In fact, a love for missions is really just a love for Christ's church; specifically loving the church in a place where the church is not yet gathered, is small, or is weak. Missionaries simply uproot their love for the church from one place so as to plant that same love somewhere else.

Sometimes people think that the profile of a missionary is something like a Christian version of Indiana Jones—a Bible-carrying adventurer. In reality, the best missionaries are just church-loving, gospel-sharing Christians—Christians who have a proven track record of bearing fruit in and through their local churches.

If You're Not Going to Be a Missionary, You Still Might Want to Consider Moving Overseas

I don't have any more "it depends" principles to offer. I'm sure there are other considerations for your life that you'll need to work through with your family and with pastors who love you and the gospel.

If after reading this book you're convinced that you *shouldn't* be a missionary, I want you to still consider moving somewhere where faithful missionaries are laboring.

Let me explain: I assume that about 99 percent of faithful Christians won't ever become missionaries. But there is still amazing, strategic work that God might do through you for the gospel for the sake of the nations.

Christians often carry around the strange idea that if they don't have an office or title then they're probably not making much of a contribution. But that's silly. Being a "normal" Christian doesn't mean you're unimportant. Yes, a pastor has a particular role with specific qualifications that most Christians won't have. And in the same way, a missionary has a particular role with specific qualifications that most Christians won't have. But we serve a God who is pleased to accomplish great things in ordinary ways with ordinary people doing ordinary things. And that, my friend, could be you.

Attach yourself to the ministry of a healthy, Bible-preaching church and through that church be a part of something glorious—the display of God's wisdom to the universe. I'm not being over the top here. That's what God himself says in Ephesians 3:10: This is "so that through the church the manifold wisdom of God might now be made known to the rulers and authorities in the heavenly places."

But maybe . . . just maybe . . . you could reorganize your life to be a faithful church member in a place where there are almost no churches and very few Christians. How exciting might that be?

In the country where I pastor, folks estimate that the population is about 0.02 percent Christians. Put another way, if you walked down the street in my town you'd need to say "Good morning" to five thousand people to have a chance of having said "Good morning" to just one Christian. Living in a place like that can be hard, but it's also exhilarating! What a great place to display the light of the gospel through a local church community. There are lots of places like this around the world.

Like many other pastors of churches in places like this, we long for more faithful Christians to just come and plant their lives in a local church here. Some might come with a job or come to study at a local university. Others might choose to use their retirement income to settle in a place with few Christians (and, yes, far from grandkids) for the sake of the health of a church and the glory of Christ. Still others might have online jobs they could do from anywhere. So why not do your online job from a place where missionaries struggle to get visas and few Christians live? People who uproot their lives to simply join and strengthen a local church in a gospel-impoverished city are precious. We could use thousands more folks like that.

———

Let me sum up.

If you've got the gifts and the character to serve as a lead missionary and the desire to do so, I'd encourage you to talk to mature leaders in your church about your desire. The church needs more qualified men leading out in gospel work and planting churches all over the world.

If you're not an elder-qualified man, but you're a man or woman who wants to come alongside someone in that role and help them, again I would encourage you to talk to a pastor in your church. Ask them to help you consider if it would be wise to pursue that path.

If you want to keep being a "normal" Christian working a normal job and serving in a local church, that's wonderful! Those acts also honor Jesus and commend the gospel, and your life is still part of God's plan to bless the nations. But you might also consider uprooting and living that "normal" Christian life in a local church in a place where Christians are as rare as diamonds. Again, if that's you, talk to a church leader about that possibility.

But most of all, whoever you are and whatever your answer to the question, "Should I be a missionary," I'd encourage you to just get busy doing good things. If you're not sure you're a Christian then get serious about investigating the claims of Jesus from the Bible. And if you are a Christian, then give yourself to serving Jesus in the fellowship of a faithful, Bible-loving local church. As you do this, maybe you will find a passion to serve his church one way or another in a place with less gospel access than where you currently live. But for now, whatever you think about missions and missionaries, there is so much good you can do where you are; let's just get on with it.

Recommended Resource

Andy Johnson, *Missions: How the Local Church Goes Global* (Wheaton, IL: Crossway, 2017).

Notes

1. When possible, personal stories in this booklet are shared with permission from those involved, and some names have been changed for privacy.
2. See J. H. Bavinck, *An Introduction to the Science of Missions*, trans. David Hugh Freeman (Philadelphia: P&R, 1960), 155–59.
3. Charles Bridges, *The Christian Ministry* (Edinburgh: Banner of Truth, 2005), 76.

Scripture Index

9Marks

Building Healthy Churches

9Marks exists to equip church leaders with
a biblical vision and practical resources
for displaying God's glory to the nations
through healthy churches.

To that end, we want to see churches
characterized by these nine marks
of health:

1. Expositional Preaching
2. Gospel Doctrine
3. A Biblical Understanding of
   Conversion and Evangelism
4. Biblical Church Membership
5. Biblical Church Discipline
6. A Biblical Concern for
   Discipleship and Growth
7. Biblical Church Leadership
8. A Biblical Understanding
   of the Practice of Prayer
9. A Biblical Understanding and
   Practice of Missions

Find all our Crossway titles
and other resources at
9Marks.org.

IX 9Marks Church Questions

Providing ordinary Christians with sound and
accessible biblical teaching by answering
common questions about church life.

For more information, visit crossway.org.